The Tabernacle of Unity

Bahá'u'lláh's Responses to Mánikchí Ṣáḥib and Other Writings

The Tabernacle of Unity

Bahá'u'lláh's Responses to Mánikchí Ṣáḥib and Other Writings

Bahá'í World Centre

ISBN 0-85398-969-9

CONTENTS

Erratum

On page i, line 3, "1851" should read "1852".

INTRODUCTION

From the birth of the Bahá'í Revelation in a subterranean dungeon in Ṭihrán where its Author was confined in 1851, the Faith of Bahá'u'lláh has rapidly grown, in ever-widening circles, beyond the social and religious matrix of its inception. Among the first individuals outside the Islamic community to be attracted to its teachings, presaging the flow of people of all faiths and origins into its universal embrace, were Zoroastrians in Persia and India. To this group Bahá'u'lláh addressed a number of Tablets, several of which are presented here for the first time in full authorized translations.

Prominent among these works is Bahá'u'lláh's Tablet to Mánikchí Ṣáḥib. Mánikchí Limjí Hataria (1813–1890), also known as Mánikchí Ṣáḥib, was born in India of Zoroastrian parents. An able diplomat and devoted adherent of his ancestral religion, Mánikchí Ṣáḥib was appointed, in 1854, as an emissary on behalf of the Parsees of India to assist their coreligionists in Iran, who were suffering under the repressive policies of the Qájár monarchs. In that same year he attained the presence of Bahá'u'lláh in Baghdad. Although maintaining to the end of his life allegiance to the Zoroastrian faith, he was attracted to the teachings of the new religion and, moved by the sacrifice of its early martyrs, became a lifelong admirer. From 1876 to 1882 he employed the eminent Bahá'í scholar Mírzá Abu'l-Faḍl as his personal secretary, and the latter acted as his intermediary with Bahá'u'lláh in relaying the questions that led to the revelation of two Tablets of far-reaching significance.

The first Tablet, known as the Lawḥ-i-Mánikchí Ṣáḥib, is celebrated for its striking and well-known passages epitomizing the universality of Bahá'u'lláh's prophetic claim. Revealed, at Mánikchí Ṣáḥib's bold request, in pure Persian, the Tablet responds to the questions he had raised and proclaims some of the central tenets of the Faith of Bahá'u'lláh: "Be anxiously concerned with the needs of the age ye live in, and centre your deliberations on its exigencies and requirements." "Turn your faces from the darkness of estrangement to the effulgent light of the daystar of unity." "Ye are the fruits of one tree, and the leaves of one branch." "[W]hatsoever leadeth to the decline of ignorance and the increase of knowledge hath been, and will ever remain, approved in the sight of the Lord of creation."

As inferred from the contents of a second Tablet, Mánikchí Ṣáḥib was not entirely satisfied with this reply, having anticipated a more expansive discussion of his specific questions. Bahá'u'lláh's further reply is contained in a lengthy Tablet, revealed on 14 Sha'bán 1299 (1 July 1882) in the voice of His amanuensis Mírzá Áqá Ján. The Tablet is addressed to Mírzá Abu'l-Faḍl, but a lengthy portion of it addresses Mánikchí Ṣáḥib's questions. Bahá'u'lláh states at the outset that he had "failed to consider the matter closely, for otherwise he would have readily admitted that not a single point was omitted", and explains that out of wisdom his questions had not been directly answered, but that even so, "the answers were provided in a language of marvellous concision and clarity". Throughout the remainder of the Tablet, the text of each of Mánikchí Ṣáḥib's questions is successively quoted and detailed replies are given to each, in some cases connecting the questions to the universal principles enunciated in the first Tablet.

The Tablet is noteworthy for its discussion of a range of questions regarding the tenets of both Abrahamic and non-Abrahamic religions, as understood by Mánikchí Ṣáḥib, including the nature of creation, the connection between faith and reason, the reconciliation of the differences that exist among the laws and ordinances of various religions, their respective claims to exclusivity and their differing degrees of eagerness to welcome others into their fold. Bahá'u'lláh's responses emphasize that which is right and true in the various doctrines and beliefs under examination, rather than discarding them outright for inaccuracy or insufficiency.

Included here as well with these two major works are the Lawḥ-i-Haft Pursish (Tablet of the Seven Questions), addressed to Ustád Javán-Mard, a prominent early Bahá'í of Zoroastrian background and former student of Mánikchí Ṣáḥib, and two other Tablets also revealed to believers of the same origin. Together, these five Tablets offer a glimpse of Bahá'u'lláh's love for, and special relationship with, the followers of a religion that had arisen, many centuries before, in the same land that witnessed the birth of His own Faith.

A portion of the Lawḥ-i-Mánikc͟hí Ṣáḥib and several excerpts from the other Tablets were previously translated by Shoghi Effendi; these have been incorporated into the text of the translations and listed in the appendix.

It is hoped that the publication of this volume will enable a deeper appreciation of the fundamental principle of the oneness of religion and lend a fresh impetus to the efforts of those who strive to promote its understanding in an age that needs it more acutely with every passing day.

I

Tablet to Mánik<u>ch</u>í Ṣáḥib

(Lawḥ-i-Mánik<u>ch</u>í Ṣáḥib)

IN THE NAME OF THE ONE TRUE GOD

PRAISE BE to the all-perceiving, the ever-abiding Lord Who, from a dewdrop out of the ocean of His grace, hath reared the firmament of existence, adorned it with the stars of knowledge, and admitted man into the lofty court of insight and understanding. This dewdrop, which is the Primal Word of God, is at times called the Water of Life, inasmuch as it quickeneth with the waters of knowledge them that have perished in the wilderness of ignorance. Again it is called the Primal Light, a light born of the Sun of divine knowledge, through whose effulgence the first stirrings of existence were made plain and manifest. Such manifestations are the expressions of the grace of Him Who is the Peerless, the All-Wise. He it is who knoweth and bestoweth all. He it is who transcendeth all that hath been said or heard. 1.1

His knowledge will remain forever above the grasp of human vision and understanding and beyond the reach of human words and deeds. To the truth of this utterance existence itself and all that hath appeared therefrom bear eloquent testimony.

1.2 It is clear and evident, therefore, that the first ➔ bestowal of God is the Word, and its discoverer and recipient is the power of understanding. This Word is the foremost instructor in the school of existence and the revealer of Him Who is the Almighty. All that is seen is visible only through the light of its wisdom. All that is manifest is but a token of its knowledge. All names are but its name, and the beginning and end of all matters must needs depend upon it.

1.3 Thy letter hath reached this captive of the world in His prison. It brought joy, strengthened the ties of friendship, and renewed the memory of bygone days. Praise be to the Lord of creation Who granted us the favour of meeting in the Arabian land,[1] wherein we visited and held converse. It is Our hope that our encounter may never be forgotten nor effaced from the heart by the passage of time, but rather that, out of the seeds thus sown, the sweet herbs of friendship may spring forth and remain forever fresh and verdant for all to behold.

1.4 As to thy question concerning the heavenly Scriptures: The All-Knowing Physician hath His finger on the pulse of mankind. He perceiveth the disease, and prescribeth, in His unerring wisdom, the remedy. Every age hath its own problem, and every soul its particular aspiration. The remedy the world needeth in its present-day afflictions can never be the same as that which a subsequent age may require. Be anxiously concerned with the needs of the age ye live in, and centre your deliberations on its exigencies and requirements.

1.5 We can well perceive how the whole human race is encompassed with great, with incalculable afflictions. We see it languishing on its bed of sickness, sore-tried and disillusioned. They that are intoxicated by self-conceit have interposed themselves between it and the Divine and infallible Physician. Witness how they have entangled all men, themselves included, in the mesh of their devices. They can neither discover the cause of the disease, nor have they any knowledge of the remedy. They have conceived the straight to be crooked, and have imagined their friend an enemy.

1.6 Incline your ears to the sweet melody of this Prisoner. Arise, and lift up your voices, that haply they that are fast asleep may be awakened. Say: O ye who are as dead! The Hand of Divine bounty proffereth unto you the Water of Life. Hasten and drink your fill. Whoso hath been reborn in this Day, shall never die; whoso remaineth dead, shall never live.

1.7 Thou hast written concerning languages. Both Arabic and Persian are laudable. That which is desired of a language is that it convey the intent of the speaker, and either language can serve this purpose. And since in this day the Orb of divine knowledge hath risen in the firmament of Persia, that tongue deserveth every praise.

1.8 O friend! When the Primal Word appeared amongst men in these latter days, a number of heavenly souls recognized the voice of the Beloved and bore allegiance unto it, whilst others, finding the deeds of some to be at variance with their words, remained far removed from the spreading rays of the Sun of divine knowledge.

1.9 Say: O children of dust! He Who is the Spirit of Purity saith: In this glorious Day whatsoever can purge you from defilement and ensure your peace and tranquillity, that indeed is the straight Path,[2] the Path that leadeth unto Me. To be purged from defilement is to be cleansed of that which is injurious to man and detracteth from his high station—among which is to take undue pleasure in one's own words and deeds, notwithstanding their unworthiness. True peace and tranquillity will only be realized when every soul will have become the well-wisher of all mankind. He Who is the All-Knowing beareth Me witness: were the peoples of the world to grasp the true significance of the words of God, they would never be deprived of their portion of the ocean of His bounty. In the firmament of truth there hath never been, nor will there ever be, a brighter star than this.

The first utterance of Him Who is the All- 1.10
Wise is this: O children of dust! Turn your faces from the darkness of estrangement to the effulgent light of the daystar of unity. This is that which above all else will benefit the peoples of the earth. O friend! Upon the tree of utterance there hath never been, nor shall there ever be, a fairer leaf, and beneath the ocean of knowledge no pearl more wondrous can ever be found.

O children of understanding! If the eyelid, 1.11
however delicate, can deprive man's outer eye

from beholding the world and all that is therein, consider then what would be wrought if the veil of covetousness were to descend upon his inner eye. Say: O people! The darkness of greed and envy becloudeth the radiance of the soul even as the clouds obstruct the light of the sun. Should anyone hearken unto this utterance with a discerning ear, he will unfurl the wings of detachment and soar effortlessly in the atmosphere of true understanding.

1.12 At a time when darkness had encompassed the world, the ocean of divine favour surged and His Light was made manifest, that the doings of men might be laid bare. This, verily, is that Light which hath been foretold in the heavenly scriptures. Should the Almighty so please, the hearts of all men will be purged and purified through His goodly utterance, and the light of unity will shed its radiance upon every soul and revive the whole earth.

1.13 O people! Words must be supported by deeds, for deeds are the true test of words. Without the former, the latter can never quench the thirst of the yearning soul, nor unlock the portals of vision before the eyes of the blind. The Lord of celestial wisdom saith: A harsh word is even as a sword thrust; a gentle word as milk. The latter leadeth the children of men unto knowledge and conferreth upon them true distinction.

The Tongue of Wisdom proclaimeth: He that hath Me not is bereft of all things. Turn ye away from all that is on earth and seek none else but Me. I am the Sun of Wisdom and the Ocean of Knowledge. I cheer the faint and revive the dead. I am the guiding Light that illumineth the way. I am the royal Falcon on the arm of the Almighty. I unfold the drooping wings of every broken bird and start it on its flight. 1.14

The incomparable Friend saith: The path to freedom hath been outstretched; hasten ye thereunto. The wellspring of wisdom is overflowing; quaff ye therefrom. Say: O well-beloved ones! The tabernacle of unity hath been raised; regard ye not one another as strangers. Ye are the fruits of one tree, and the leaves of one branch. Verily I say, whatsoever leadeth to the decline of ignorance and the increase of knowledge hath been, and will ever remain, approved in the sight of the Lord of creation. Say: O people! Walk ye neath the shadow of justice and truthfulness and seek ye shelter within the tabernacle of unity. 1.15

1.16 Say: O ye that have eyes to see! The past is the mirror of the future. Gaze ye therein and be apprised thereof; perchance ye may be aided thereby to recognize the Friend and may be not the cause of His displeasure. In this day the choicest fruit of the tree of knowledge is that which serveth the welfare of humanity and safeguardeth its interests.

1.17 Say: The tongue hath been created to bear witness to My truth; defile it not with falsehood. The heart is the treasury of My mystery; surrender it not into the hand of covetous desires. We fain would hope that in this resplendent morn, when the effulgent rays of the Sun of divine knowledge have enveloped the whole earth, we may all attain unto the good pleasure of the Friend and drink our fill from the ocean of His recognition.

1.18 O friend! As hearing ears are scarce to find, the pen hath for some time remained silent in its quarters. In truth, matters have come to such a pass that silence hath taken precedence over utterance and hath come to be regarded as preferable. Say: O people! These words are being uttered in due measure, that the newly born may thrive and the tender shoot flourish. Milk should be given in suitable proportion, that the children of the world may attain to the station of maturity and abide in the court of oneness.

O friend! We came upon a pure soil and sowed therein the seeds of true understanding. Let it now be seen what the rays of the sun will do—whether they will cause these seeds to wither or to grow. Say: Through the ascendancy of God, the All-Knowing, the Incomparable, the Luminary of divine understanding hath, in this day, risen from behind the veil of the spirit, and the birds of every meadow are intoxicated with the wine of knowledge and exhilarated with the remembrance of the Friend. Well is it with them that discover and hasten unto Him! 1.19

2

Responses to questions of Mánikchí Ṣáḥib from a Tablet to Mírzá Abu'l-Faḍl

IN REGARD TO WHAT THOU hast written concerning his honour the learned Ṣáḥib, upon him be the grace of God, his state of mind and disposition are clear and evident, as is further attested by that which he hath sent. Now, as to his questions, it was not deemed advisable to refer and reply to each one individually, for the response would have run counter to wisdom and been incompatible with that which is current amongst men. Even so, in that which was revealed in his honour from the heaven of divine favour, answers were provided in a language of marvellous concision and clarity. But it appeareth that he hath failed to consider the matter closely, for otherwise he would have readily admitted that not a single point was omitted, and would have exclaimed: "This is naught but a clear and conclusive utterance!" His questions were the following. 2.1

2.2 First: "The Prophets of Mahábád, together with Zoroaster, were twenty-eight in number. Each one of them sought to exalt, rather than abrogate, the faith and religion of the others. Each one that appeared bore witness to the truth and veracity of the former law and religion and breathed no word about abolishing them. Each declared: 'We are the bearers of a Revelation from God, which We deliver unto His servants.' Some of the Hindu Prophets, however, have declared: 'We are God Himself, and it is incumbent upon the entire creation to bear allegiance unto Us. Whensoever conflict and dissension appear amongst men, We arise to quench it.' Each one that appeared announced: 'I am the same One that appeared in the beginning.' The latter Prophets such as David, Abraham, Moses and Jesus confirmed the truth of the Prophets gone before them, but said: 'Such was the law in the past, but in this day the law is that which I proclaim.' The Arabian Prophet, however, hath said: 'Through My appearance every law hath proven to be unsound and no law holdeth but Mine.' Which of these creeds is acceptable and which of these leaders is to be preferred?"

It should first be noted that in one sense the stations of the Prophets of God differ one from another. For instance, consider Moses. He brought forth a Book and established ordinances, whilst a number of the Prophets and Messengers who arose after Him were charged with the promulgation of His laws, insofar as they remained consonant with the needs of the age. The books and chronicles annexed to the Torah bear eloquent testimony to this truth. 2.3

Regarding the statement ascribed to the Author of the Qur'án: "Through My appearance every law and religion hath proven to be unsound and no law holdeth but Mine", no such words were ever uttered by that Source and Fount of divine wisdom. Nay rather, He confirmed that which had been sent down before from the empyrean of the Divine Will unto the Prophets and Messengers of God. He saith, exalted be His utterance: "Alif. Lám. Mím. God! There is no God but Him, the Living, the Ever-Abiding. He it is Who hath sent down to Thee the Book through the power of truth, confirming those which preceded it. He revealed aforetime the Torah and the Evangel as a guidance unto men, and He hath now revealed the 2.4

Qur'án...."[3] He, moreover, hath asserted that all the Prophets have proceeded from God and have returned unto Him. Viewed in this light, they are all as one and the same Being, inasmuch as they have not uttered a word, brought a message, or revealed a cause, of their own accord. Nay, all that they have said hath proceeded from the one true God, exalted be His glory. They have all summoned men unto the Supreme Horizon and imparted the tidings of eternal life. Thus the diverse statements recounted by his honour the Ṣáḥib are to be seen as concordant letters, that is, letters that form a single word.

2.5 Concerning the question: "Which of these creeds is acceptable and which of these leaders is to be preferred?", this is the station wherein the following blessed words shine resplendent as the sun: "No distinction do We make between any of His Messengers",[4] while the verse "Some of the Apostles We have caused to excel the others"[5] pertaineth to the other station of which We have already made mention. Indeed, the answer to all that his honour the Ṣáḥib hath asked lieth enshrined within this all-embracing, this weighty and incomparable utterance, hallowed and exalted be His word: "As to thy question concerning the heavenly Scriptures: The All-Knowing Physician hath His finger on the pulse of mankind. He perceiveth the disease, and prescribeth, in His unerring wisdom, the remedy. Every age hath its own problem, and every soul its particular aspiration. The remedy the world needeth in its present-day afflictions can never be the same as that which a subsequent age may require. Be anxiously concerned with the needs of the age ye live in, and centre your deliberations on its exigencies and requirements."[6] Every fair-minded soul will testify that these words are to be viewed as a mirror of the knowledge of God, wherein all that hath been inquired is clearly and conspicuously reflected. Blessed is he who hath been endowed with seeing eyes by God, the All-Knowing, the All-Wise.

Another question raised by the distinguished 2.6
Ṣáḥib is the following: "'There are four schools of thought in the world. One school affirmeth that all the visible worlds, from atoms to suns, constitute God Himself and that naught can be seen but Him. Another school claimeth that God is that Essence that must of necessity exist, that His Messengers are the intermediaries between Him and His creatures, and that

their mission is to lead humanity unto Him. Yet another school holdeth that the stars were created by the Necessary Being,[7] whilst all other things are their effect and outcome. These things continually appear and disappear, even as the minute creatures that are generated in a pool of water. A further school maintaineth that the Necessary Being hath fashioned Nature through whose effect and agency all things, from atoms to suns, appear and disappear without beginning or end. What need then for an account or reckoning? As the grass groweth with the coming of the rain and vanisheth thereafter, so it is with all things. If the Prophets and the kings have instituted laws and ordinances, the proponents of this school argue, this hath merely been for the sake of preserving the civil order and regulating human society. The Prophets and the kings, however, have acted in different ways: the former have said 'God hath spoken thus' that the people might submit and obey, whilst the latter have resorted to the sword and the cannon. Which of these four schools is approved in the sight of God?"

2.7 The answer to all this falleth under the purview of the first utterance that hath streamed forth from the tongue of the All-Merciful. By God! It embraceth and comprehendeth all that hath been mentioned. He saith: "Be anxiously concerned with the needs of the age ye live in, and centre your deliberations on its exigencies and requirements." For in this day He Who is the Lord of Revelation hath appeared and He Who spoke on Sinai is calling aloud. Whatsoever He may ordain is the surest foundation for the mansions reared in the cities of human knowledge and wisdom. Whoso holdeth fast unto it will be reckoned in the eyes of the Almighty among them that are endued with insight.

These sublime words have streamed forth 2.8
from the Pen of the Most High. He saith, exalted be His glory: "This is the day of vision, for the countenance of God is shining resplendent above the horizon of Manifestation. This is the day of hearing, for the call of God hath been raised. It behoveth everyone in this day to uphold and proclaim that which hath been revealed by Him Who is the Author of all scripture, the Dayspring of revelation, the Fount of knowledge and the Source of divine wisdom." It is thus clear and evident that the reply to his question hath been revealed in the kingdom of

utterance by Him Who is the Exponent of the knowledge of the All-Merciful. Happy are they that understand!

2.9 As to the four schools mentioned above, it is clear and evident that the second standeth closer to righteousness.[8] For the Apostles and Messengers of God have ever been the channels of His abounding grace, and whatsoever man hath received from God hath been through the intermediary of those Embodiments of holiness and Essences of detachment, those Repositories of His knowledge and Exponents of His Cause. One can, however, provide a justification for the tenets of the other schools, for in a sense all things have ever been and shall ever remain the manifestations of the names and attributes of God.

2.10 As to the Ṣáḥib's reference to the kings, they are indeed the manifestations of the name of God "the Almighty" and the revealers of His name "the All-Powerful". The vesture that beseemeth their glorious temples is justice. Should they become adorned therewith, mankind will partake of perfect tranquillity and infinite blessings.

2.11 Whoso hath quaffed of the wine of divine knowledge will indeed be able to answer such questions with clear and perspicuous proofs from the world without and with manifest and luminous evidences from the world within. A different Cause, however, hath appeared in this day and a different discourse is required. Indeed, with the inception of the year nine the time for questions and answers came to an end. Thus He, hallowed and magnified be His name, saith: "This is not the day for any man to question his Lord. When thou hearest the call of God voiced by Him Who is the Dayspring of grandeur, cry out: 'Here am I, O Lord of all names! Here am I, O Maker of the heavens! I testify that Thou hast revealed Thyself and hast revealed whatsoever Thou didst desire at Thine Own behest. Thou, in truth, art the Lord of strength and might.'"

The answer to all that the distinguished Ṣáḥib 2.12
hath asked is clear and evident. The intent of that which was sent down in his honour from the heaven of divine providence was that he might give ear to the wondrous melodies of the Dove of Eternity and the gentle murmuring of the inhabitants of the most exalted Paradise, and that he might perceive the sweetness of the call and set foot upon the path.

2.13 One day the Tongue of Glory uttered a word in regard to the Ṣáḥib indicating that he may erelong be aided to perform a deed that would immortalize his name. When his letter was received in His holy and exalted Court, He said: "O Servant in attendance! Although his honour Mánikchí hath written only to ask concerning the sayings of others, yet from His letter We inhale the sweet savours of affection. Beseech the one true God to graciously aid him to do His will and pleasure. His might, in truth, is equal to all things." From this utterance of the All-Merciful there wafteth a fragrant breath. He, verily, is the All-Knowing, the All-Informed.

2.14 Another inquiry made by him is the following: "The laws of Islam are based on religious principles and jurisprudence,[9] but in the Mahábád and Hindu religions there are only principles, and all laws, even those regarding the drinking of water or giving and taking in marriage, are considered a part of these principles, as are all other matters of human life. Kindly indicate which view is acceptable in the sight of God, exalted be His mention."

2.15 Religious principles have various degrees and stations. The root of all principles and the cornerstone of all foundations hath ever been, and shall remain, the recognition of God. And these days are indeed the vernal season of the recognition of the All-Merciful. Whatsoever proceedeth in this day from the Repository of His Cause and the Manifestation of His Self is, in truth, the fundamental principle unto which all must bear allegiance.

The answer to this question is also embod- 2.16
ied in these blessed, these weighty and exalted words: "Be anxiously concerned with the needs of the age ye live in, and centre your deliberations on its exigencies and requirements." For this day is the Lord of all days, and whatsoever hath been revealed therein by the Source of divine Revelation is the truth and the essence of all principles. This day may be likened to a sea and all other days to gulfs and channels that have branched therefrom. That which is uttered and revealed in this day is the foundation, and is accounted as the Mother Book and the Source of all utterance. Although every day is associated with God, magnified be His glory, yet these days have been singled out and adorned with the ornament of intimate association with Him, for they have been extolled in the books of the

Chosen Ones of God, as well as of some of His Prophets, as the "Day of God". In a sense this day and that which appeareth therein are to be regarded as the primary principles, while all other days and whatsoever appeareth in them are to be viewed as the secondary ordinances deduced therefrom, and which as such are subordinate and relative. For instance, attending the mosque is secondary with respect to the recognition of God, for the former is dependent upon and conditioned by the latter. As to the principles current amongst the divines of this age, these are merely a set of rules which they have devised and from which they infer, each according to his own opinions and inclinations, the ordinances of God.

2.17 Consider for example the question of immediate compliance or postponement. God, exalted be His glory, saith: "Eat and drink…."[10] Now, it is not known whether this ordinance must be complied with immediately or if its execution may be justifiably postponed. Some believe that it may be decided by external circumstances. Once one of the distinguished divines of Najaf set out to visit the Shrine of Imám Ḥusayn, peace be upon Him, accompanied by a number of his pupils. In the course of their journey they were waylaid by a group of Bedouin. The aforementioned divine immediately handed over all his possessions. Whereupon his pupils exclaimed: "Your eminence hath always favoured postponement in such matters. What prompteth you now to act with such haste?" Pointing to the spears of the Bedouin, he replied: "The force of external circumstances, my friends!"

The founder of the principles of Islamic juris- 2.18
prudence was Abú-Ḥanífih, who was a prominent leader of the Sunnis. Such principles had existed in former times as well, as hath already been mentioned. In this day, however, the approval or rejection of all things dependeth wholly upon the Word of God. These differences are not worthy of mention. The eye of divine mercy casteth its glance upon all that is past. It behoveth us to mention them only in favourable terms, for they do not contradict that which is essential. This servant testifieth to his ignorance and beareth witness that all knowledge is with God, the Help in Peril, the Self-Subsisting.

Whatsoever runneth counter to the Teach- 2.19
ings in this day is rejected, for the Sun of Truth is shining resplendent above the horizon of

knowledge. Happy are they who, with the waters of divine utterance, have cleansed their hearts from all allusions, whisperings and suggestions, and who have fixed their gaze upon the Dayspring of Glory. This, indeed, is the most gracious favour and the purest bounty. Whosoever hath attained thereunto hath attained unto all good, for otherwise the knowledge of aught else but God hath never proven, nor shall it ever prove, profitable unto men.

2.20 That which was mentioned in connection with religious principles and secondary ordinances referreth to the pronouncements which the divines of various religions have made, each according to his own capacity. At present, however, it behoveth us to follow His injunction to "leave them to their vain disputes".[11] He, verily, speaketh the truth and leadeth the way. The decree is God's, the Almighty, the All-Bounteous.

2.21 Another of his questions: "Some maintain that whatsoever is in accordance with the dictates of nature and of the intellect must needs be both permissible and compulsory in the divine law, and conversely that one should refrain from observing that which is incompatible with these standards. Others believe that whatsoever hath been enjoined by the divine law and its blessed Author should be accepted without rational proof or natural evidence and obeyed without question or reservation, such as the march between Safa and Marwah, the stoning of the pillar of Jamrah,[12] the washing of one's feet during ablutions, and so on. Kindly indicate which of these positions is acceptable."

Intellect hath various degrees. As a dis- 2.22
cussion of the pronouncements made by the philosophers in this connection would pass beyond the scope of our discourse, we have refrained from mentioning them. It is nonetheless indisputably clear and evident that the minds of men have never been, nor shall they ever be, of equal capacity. The Perfect Intellect alone can provide true guidance and direction. Thus were these sublime words revealed by the Pen of the Most High, exalted be His glory, in response to this question: "The Tongue of Wisdom proclaimeth: He that hath Me not is bereft of all things. Turn ye away from all that is on earth and seek none else but Me. I am the Sun of Wisdom and the Ocean of Knowledge. I cheer the faint and revive the dead. I am the

guiding Light that illumineth the way. I am the royal Falcon on the arm of the Almighty. I unfold the drooping wings of every broken bird and start it on its flight."[13]

2.23 Consider how clearly the answer hath been revealed from the heaven of divine knowledge. Blessed are those who ponder it, who reflect upon it, and who apprehend its meaning! By the Intellect mentioned above is meant the universal divine Mind. How often hath it been observed that certain human minds, far from being a source of guidance, have become as fetters upon the feet of the wayfarers and prevented them from treading the straight Path! The lesser intellect being thus circumscribed, one must search after Him Who is the ultimate Source of knowledge and strive to recognize Him. And should one come to acknowledge that Source round Whom every mind doth revolve, then whatsoever He should ordain is the expression of the dictates of a consummate wisdom. His very Being, even as the sun, is distinct from all else beside Him. The whole duty of man is to recognize Him; once this hath been achieved, then whatsoever He may please to ordain is binding and in full accordance with the requirements of divine wisdom. Thus have ordinances and prohibitions of every kind been laid down by the Prophets of the past, even unto the earliest times.

Certain deeds that are undertaken in this day 2.24
are intended to emblazon the name of God, and the Pen of the Most High hath fixed a recompense for those who perform them. Indeed, should any soul breathe but a fleeting breath for the sake of God, his recompense will become manifest, as attested by this mighty verse which was sent down from the empyrean of the Divine Will to the Lord of Mecca,[14] blessed and glorified be He: "We did not appoint that which Thou wouldst have to be the Qiblih, but that We might know him who followeth the Apostle from him who turneth on his heels."[15]

Were anyone to meditate upon this blessed 2.25
and transcendent Revelation and to ponder the verses that have been sent down, he would readily bear witness that the one true God is immeasurably exalted above His creatures, and that the knowledge of all things hath ever been and shall ever remain with Him. Every fair-minded soul, moreover, will testify that whosoever faileth to embrace the truth of this most great Revelation will find himself powerless

and incapable of establishing the validity of any other cause or creed. And as to those who have deprived themselves of the robe of justice and arisen to promote the cause of iniquity, they shall give voice to that which the exponents of hatred and fanaticism have uttered from time immemorial. The knowledge of all things is with God, the All-Knowing, the All-Informed.

2.26 One day when this servant was in His presence, I was asked: "O servant in attendance! Wherewith art thou engaged?" "I am penning a reply", I answered, "to his honour Mírzá Abu'l-Faḍl." I was bidden: "Write to Mírzá Abu'l-Faḍl, may My glory be upon him, and say: 'Matters have come to such a pass that the people of the world have grown accustomed to iniquity and flee from fair-mindedness. A divine Manifestation Who hath extolled and magnified the one true God, exalted be His glory, Who hath borne witness to His knowledge and confessed that His Essence is sanctified above all things and exalted beyond every comparison—such a Manifestation hath been called at various times a worshipper of the sun or a fire-worshipper. How numerous are those sublime Manifestations and Revealers of the Divine of Whose stations the people remain wholly unaware, of Whose grace they are utterly deprived, nay, God forbid, Whom they curse and revile!

"'One of the great Prophets Whom the 2.27
foolish ones of Persia in this day reject uttered these sublime words: "The sun is but a dense and spherical mass. It deserveth not to be called God or the Almighty. For the almighty Lord is He Whom no human comprehension can ever conceive, Whom no earthly knowledge can circumscribe, and Whose Essence none hath ever been or shall ever be able to fathom." Consider how eloquently, how solemnly He hath affirmed the very truth that God is proclaiming in this day. And yet He is not even deemed a believer by these abject and foolish ones, let alone seen as possessed of a sublime station! In another connection He said: "All existence hath appeared from His existence, and were it not for God, no creature would have ever existed and been attired with the raiment of being." May the Lord shield us all from the wickedness of such as have disputed the truth of God and of His loved ones and turned away from that Dayspring whereunto all the Books of God, the Help in Peril, the Self-Subsisting, have testified.'"

2.28 From that which hath been mentioned, it is clear that not every intellect can be the criterion of truth. The truly wise are, in the first place, the Chosen Ones of God, magnified be His glory—they Whom He hath singled out to be the Treasuries of His knowledge, the Repositories of His Revelation, the Daysprings of His authority and the Dawning-places of His wisdom, they Whom He hath made His representatives on earth and through Whom He revealeth that which He hath purposed. Whoso turneth unto them hath turned unto God, and whoso turneth away shall not be remembered in the presence of God, the All-Knowing, the All-Wise.

2.29 The universal criterion is that which hath just been mentioned. Whosoever attaineth thereunto, that is, who recognizeth and acknowledgeth the Dawning-place of God's Revelation, will be recorded in the Book of God among them that are endued with understanding. Otherwise he is naught but an ignorant soul, though he believe himself to be possessed of every wisdom. Now, were a person to see himself standing in the presence of God, were he to sanctify his soul from earthly attachments and evil intentions, and reflect upon that which hath been revealed in this most great Revelation from its inception to this day, he would readily testify that every detached soul, every perfect mind, sanctified being, attentive ear, penetrating eye, eloquent tongue, and joyous and radiant heart circleth round and boweth down, nay prostrateth itself in submission, before the mighty throne of God.

Another of his questions is this: "Among the 2.30
Manifestations of the past one hath, in His time, allowed the eating of beef while another hath forbidden it; one hath permitted the eating of pork whereas another hath proscribed it. Thus do their ordinances differ. I entreat the True One, exalted be His name, to graciously specify the appropriate religious prohibitions."

A direct reply and detailed explanation of 2.31
this matter would have overstepped the bounds of wisdom, inasmuch as people of diverse faiths associate with the distinguished Ṣáḥib and a direct reply would have contravened the laws of Islam. The answer was therefore sent down from the heaven of the Divine Will in an implicit manner. Indeed the statement in the first passage where He saith: "The All-Knowing Physician hath His finger on the pulse of mankind" was, and remaineth, the answer to his

question. He further saith: "Be anxiously concerned with the needs of the age ye live in, and centre your deliberations on its exigencies and requirements." That is, fix your gaze upon the commandments of God, for whatsoever He should ordain in this day and pronounce as lawful is indeed lawful and representeth the very truth. It is incumbent upon all to turn their gaze towards the Cause of God and to observe that which hath dawned above the horizon of His Will, since it is through the potency of His name that the banner of "He doeth what He willeth" hath been unfurled and the standard of "He ordaineth what He pleaseth" hath been raised aloft. For instance, were He to pronounce water itself to be unlawful, it would indeed become unlawful, and the converse holdeth equally true. For upon no thing hath it been inscribed "this is lawful" or "this is unlawful"; nay rather, whatsoever hath been or will be revealed is by virtue of the Word of God, exalted be His glory.

2.32 These matters are sufficiently clear and require no further elaboration. Even so, certain groups believe that all the ordinances current amongst them are unalterable, that they have ever been valid, and that they will forever remain so. Consider a further passage, glorified and exalted be He: "These words are being uttered in due measure, that the newly born may thrive and the tender shoot flourish. Milk must be given in suitable proportion, that the children of the world may attain to the station of maturity and abide in the court of oneness."[16] For instance, some believe that wine hath ever been and shall remain forbidden. Now, were one to inform them that it might one day be made lawful, they would arise in protest and opposition. In truth, the people of the world have yet not grasped the meaning of "He doeth whatsoever He willeth", nor have they comprehended the significance of Supreme Infallibility. The suckling child must be nourished with milk. If it be given meat it will assuredly perish, and this would be naught but sheer injustice and unwisdom. Blessed are they that understand. Supreme Infallibility, as I once heard from His blessed lips, is reserved exclusively to the Manifestations of the Cause of God and the Exponents of His Revelation. This matter is mentioned but briefly, for time is short and as scarce as the legendary phoenix.

2.33 Yet another question: "According to the teachings of the Mahábád and Hindu religions, should a person of whatever faith or nation, of whatever colour, appearance, character or condition, be disposed to associate with you, ye should show forth kindness and treat him as a brother. But in other religions this is not so: their followers ill-treat and oppress the adherents of other faiths, consider their persecution as an act of worship, and regard their kindred and their possessions as lawful unto themselves. Which approach is acceptable in the sight of God?"

2.34 The former statement hath ever been and will continue to be true. It is not permissible to contend with anyone, nor is it acceptable in the sight of God to ill-treat or oppress any soul. Time and again have these sublime words streamed from the Pen of the Most High, blessed and exalted be He: "O ye children of men! The fundamental purpose animating the Faith of God and His Religion is to safeguard the interests and promote the unity of the human race, and to foster the spirit of love and fellowship amongst men. Suffer it not to become a source of dissension and discord, of hate and enmity."

This subject hath already been set forth and explained in various Tablets.

It behoveth him who expoundeth the Word of God to deliver it with the utmost goodwill, kindness, and compassion. As to him that embraceth the truth and is honoured with recognizing Him, his name shall be recorded in the Crimson Book among the inmates of the all-highest Paradise. Should a soul fail, however, to accept the truth, it is in no wise permissible to contend with him. In another connection He saith: "Blessed and happy is he that ariseth to promote the best interests of the peoples and kindreds of the earth." Likewise He saith: "The people of Bahá should soar high above the peoples of the world." In matters of religion every form of fanaticism, hatred, dissension and strife is strictly forbidden. 2.35

In this day a Luminary hath dawned above the horizon of divine providence, upon whose brow the Pen of Glory hath inscribed these exalted words: "We have called you into being to show forth love and fidelity, not animosity and hatred." Likewise, on another occasion, He—exalted and glorified be His name—hath revealed the following words in the Persian 2.36

tongue, words through which the hearts of the well-favoured and the sincere amongst His servants are consumed, the manifold pursuits of men are harmonized, and mankind is illumined by the light of divine unity and enabled to turn towards the Dayspring of divine knowledge: "The incomparable Friend saith: The path to freedom hath been outstretched; hasten ye thereunto. The wellspring of wisdom is overflowing; quaff ye therefrom. Say: O well-beloved ones! The tabernacle of unity hath been raised; regard ye not one another as strangers. Ye are the fruits of one tree, and the leaves of one branch."[17]

2.37 Justice, which consisteth in rendering each his due, dependeth upon and is conditioned by two words: reward and punishment. From the standpoint of justice, every soul should receive the reward of his actions, inasmuch as the peace and prosperity of the world depend thereon, even as He saith, exalted be His glory: "The structure of world stability and order hath been reared upon, and will continue to be sustained by, the twin pillars of reward and punishment." In brief, every circumstance requireth a different utterance and every occasion calleth for a different course of action. Blessed are they that have arisen to serve God, who speak forth wholly for His sake, and who return unto Him.

Another of his questions: "Hindus and Zoroastrians do not admit or welcome outsiders who wish to join their ranks. Christians welcome those who decide of their own accord to embrace their religion, but make no effort and exert no pressure to this end. Muslims and Jews, however, insist upon it, enjoin it upon others, and, should anyone refuse, grow hostile and regard it as lawful to seize his kindred and possessions. Which approach is acceptable in the sight of God?" 2.38

The children of men are all brothers, and the prerequisites of brotherhood are manifold. Among them is that one should wish for one's brother that which one wisheth for oneself. Therefore, it behoveth him who is the recipient of an inward or outward gift or who partaketh of the bread of heaven to inform and invite his friends with the utmost love and kindness. If they respond favourably, his object is attained; otherwise he should leave them to themselves without contending with them or uttering a word that would cause the least sadness. This is the undoubted truth, and aught else is unworthy and unbecoming. 2.39

2.40 The distinguished Ṣáḥib, may God graciously aid him, hath written that the Hindus and Zoroastrians do not permit or welcome outsiders who wish to join their ranks. This runneth counter to the purpose underlying the advent of the Messengers of God and to that which hath been revealed in their Books. For those Who have appeared at God's behest have been entrusted with the guidance and education of all people. How could they debar a seeker from the object of his quest, or forbid a wayfarer from the desire of his heart? The fire-temples of the world stand as eloquent testimony to this truth. In their time they summoned, with burning zeal, all the inhabitants of the earth to Him Who is the Spirit of purity.

2.41 He hath moreover written that Christians welcome those who decide of their own accord to embrace their religion, but make no effort and exert no pressure to this end. This, however, is a misconception. For the Christians have exerted and continue to exert the utmost effort in teaching their faith. Their church organizations have an expenditure of about thirty million. Their missionaries have scattered far and wide throughout the globe and are assiduously engaged in teaching Christianity. Thus have they compassed the world. How numerous the schools and the churches they have founded to instruct children, yet their unavowed aim is that these children, as they acquire an education, may also become acquainted in their early years with the Gospel of Jesus Christ, and that the unsullied mirrors of their hearts may thus reflect that which their teachers have purposed. Indeed the followers of no other religion are as intent upon the propagation of their faith as the Christians.

In brief, what is right and true in this day 2.42
and acceptable before His Throne is that which was mentioned at the outset. All men have been called into being for the betterment of the world. It behoveth every soul to arise and serve his brethren for the sake of God. Should a brother of his embrace the truth, he should rejoice that the latter hath attained unto everlasting favour. Otherwise he should implore God to guide him without manifesting the least trace of animosity or ill-feeling towards him. The reins of command are in the grasp of God. He doeth what He willeth and ordaineth as He pleaseth. He, verily, is the Almighty, the All-Praised.

2.43 We beseech the one true God, magnified be His glory, to enable us to recognize Him Whose unerring wisdom pervadeth all things and that we may acknowledge His truth. For once one hath recognized Him and borne witness to His Reality, one will no longer be troubled by the idle fancies and vain imaginings of men. The divine Physician hath the pulse of mankind within His almighty grasp. At one time He may well deem fit to sever certain infected limbs, that the disease may not spread to other parts of the body. This would be the very essence of mercy and compassion, and to none is given the right to object, for He is indeed the All-Knowing, the All-Seeing.

2.44 Another of his questions: "In the Mahábád and Zoroastrian religions it is said: 'Our faith and religion is superior to every other. The other Prophets and the religions they have instituted are true, but they occupy different stations before God, even as, in the court of a king, there is a gradation of ranks from the prime minister to the common soldier. Whosoever wisheth, let him keep the precepts of his religion.' Nor do they impose upon any soul. The Hindus claim that whosoever partaketh of meat, for whatever reason or under whatever circumstances, shall never catch a glimpse of Paradise. The followers of Muḥammad, Jesus and Moses maintain that a similar fate awaiteth those who fail to bear allegiance to their religions. Which belief is favoured by God, glorified be His mention?"

Regarding their statement that "our faith and religion is superior to every other", by this is meant such Prophets as have appeared before them. Viewed from one perspective these holy Souls are one: the first among them is the same as the last, and the last is the same as the first. All have proceeded from God, unto Him have they summoned all men, and unto Him have they returned. This theme hath been set forth in the Book of Certitude, which is indeed the cynosure of all books, and which streamed from the Pen of Glory in the early years of this Most Great Revelation. Blessed is he that hath beheld it and pondered its contents for the love of God, the Lord of creation. 2.45

Concerning the remark attributed to the Hindus that whosoever partaketh of meat shall never catch a glimpse of Paradise, this runneth counter to their other assertion that all the Prophets are true. For if their truth be established, then it is absurd to claim that their 2.46

followers will not ascend unto Paradise. One fain would ask what they intend by Paradise and what they have grasped thereof. In this day whosoever attaineth the good pleasure of the one true God, magnified be His glory, shall be remembered and accounted among the inmates of the all-highest Heaven and the most exalted Paradise, and shall partake of its benefits in all the worlds of God. By Him Who is the Desire of all men! The pen is powerless to portray this station or to expound this theme. How great the blessedness of him who hath attained unto the good-pleasure of God, and woe betide the heedless! Once the validity of a divinely appointed Prophet hath been established, to none is given the right to ask why or wherefore. Rather is it incumbent upon all to accept and obey whatsoever He saith. This is that which God hath decreed in all His Books, Scriptures and Tablets.

2.47 A further question that he hath asked: "The Hindus assert that God fashioned the Intellect in the form of a man named Brahma, Who came into this world and was the cause of its progress and development, and that all Hindus are His descendants. The followers of Zoroaster say: 'God, through the agency of the

Primal Intellect, created a man whose name is Mahábád and who is our ancestor.' They believe the modes of creation to be six in number. Two were mentioned above; the others are creation from water, earth, fire, and from bears and monkeys. The Hindus and Zoroastrians both say that they are begotten of the Intellect, and thus do not admit others into their folds. Are these assertions true or not? That wise Master is requested to indicate that which he deemeth appropriate."

The entire creation hath been called into 2.48
being through the Will of God, magnified be His glory, and peerless Adam hath been fashioned through the agency of His all-compelling Word, a Word which is the source, the wellspring, the repository, and the dawning-place of the intellect. From it all creation hath proceeded, and it is the channel of God's primal grace. None can grasp the reality of the origin of creation save God, exalted be His glory, Whose knowledge embraceth all things both before and after they come into being. Creation hath neither beginning nor end, and none hath ever unravelled its mystery. Its knowledge hath ever been, and shall remain, hidden and preserved with those Who are the Repositories of divine knowledge.

2.49 The world of existence is contingent, inasmuch as it is preceded by a cause, while essential pre-existence hath ever been, and shall remain, confined to God, magnified be His glory. This statement is being made lest one be inclined to conclude from the earlier assertion, namely that creation hath no beginning and no end, that it is pre-existent. True and essential pre-existence is exclusively reserved to God, while the pre-existence of the world is secondary and relative. All that hath been inferred about firstness, lastness and such hath in truth been derived from the sayings of the Prophets, Apostles and Chosen Ones of God.

2.50 As to the "realm of subtle entities"[18] which is often referred to, it pertaineth to the Revelation of the Prophets, and aught else is mere superstition and idle fancy. At the time of the Revelation all men are equal in rank. By reason, however, of their acceptance or rejection, rise or fall, motion or stillness, recognition or denial, they come to differ thereafter. For instance, the one true God, magnified be His glory, speaking through the intermediary of His Manifestation, doth ask: "Am I not your Lord?" Every soul that answereth "Yea, verily!" is accounted among the most distinguished of all men in the sight of God. Our meaning is that ere the Word of God is delivered, all men are deemed equal in rank and their station is one and the same. It is only thereafter that differences appear, as thou hast no doubt observed.

It is clearly established from that which hath 2.51
been mentioned that none may ever justifiably claim: "We are begotten of the Intellect, while all others stem from another origin." The truth that shineth bright and resplendent as the sun is this, that all have been created through the operation of the Divine Will and have proceeded from the same source, that all are from Him and that unto Him they shall all return. This is the meaning of that blessed verse in the Qur'án which hath issued from the Pen of the All-Merciful: "Verily, we are God's, and to Him shall we return."[19]

As is clear and evident to thee, the answer 2.52
to all of the questions mentioned above was embodied in but one of the passages revealed by the Pen of the Most High. Blessed are they who, freed from worldly matters and sanctified from idle fancies and vain imaginings, traverse the meads of divine knowledge and discern in all things the tokens of His glory.

2.53 Numerous passages have been revealed in the name of his honour the Ṣáḥib. Were he to appreciate their value and avail himself of their fruits, he would experience such joy that all the sorrows of the world would be powerless to afflict him. God grant that he may be enabled to sincerely voice, and to act in accordance with, the following words: "Say: It is God; then leave them to entertain themselves with their cavilings."[20] May he endeavour to guide those deprived souls who remain secluded in darkness and obscurity towards the light of the Sun. May he seize, through the potency of the Most Great Name, the banner that speaketh of naught save His Revelation and march at the forefront of the people of the former religions, that perchance the darkness of the world may be dispelled and the effulgent rays of the Sun of Truth may shine upon all mankind. This, in truth, is the most perfect bounty and the highest calling. Should man fail to attain unto this sublime station, where then can he find comfort and joy? What will sustain and animate him? With whom will he commune at the hour of repose, and whose name will he invoke when he riseth from slumber? Again: "Verily, we are God's, and to Him shall we return."

His last question: "Most of the Tablets that we have seen are in Arabic. However, since the Beloved in this age is of Persian descent, the Arabic tongue should be abandoned and discarded. For to this day the Arabs themselves have not understood the meaning of the Qur'án, whereas the Persian language is highly prized, lauded and admired among the dwellers of the inhabited quarter of the globe. And just as the Persian of the present day is superior to Arabic, so too is Old Persian, which is greatly favoured by the people of India and others. It would therefore be preferable if the words of God, magnified be His mention, were hereafter mainly delivered in pure Persian, since it attracteth the hearts to a greater degree. It is moreover requested that the reply to these questions be graciously written in pure Persian." 2.54

The Persian tongue is in truth exceedingly sweet and pleasing, and ever since this request was submitted in His most blessed and exalted court, numerous Tablets have been revealed in that language. As to the statement concerning the Qur'án implying that its outward meaning hath not been understood, in reality it hath been interpreted in numerous ways and translated into 2.55

countless languages. That which men have been unable to grasp are its hidden mysteries and inner meanings. And all that they have said or will say is limited in scope and should be seen as commensurate with their rank and station. For none can fathom its true meaning save God, the One, the Incomparable, the All-Knowing.

2.56 In this day He Who is the Lord, the Ruler, the Fashioner, and the Refuge of the world hath appeared. Let every ear be eager to hearken unto that which will be revealed from the kingdom of His will; let every eye be expectant to gaze upon that which will shine forth from the Daystar of knowledge and wisdom. By Him Who is the Desire of the world! This is the day for eyes to see and for ears to hear, for hearts to perceive and for tongues to speak forth. Blessed are they that have attained thereunto; blessed are they that have sought after and recognized it! This is the day whereon every man may accede unto everlasting honour, for whatsoever hath streamed forth from the Pen of Glory in regard to any soul is adorned with the ornament of immortality. Again, blessed are they that have attained thereunto!

2.57 The distinguished Ṣáḥib hath written: "Since the Beloved in this age is of Persian descent, the Arabic tongue should be abandoned and discarded." In this connection these sublime words issued from the Pen of the Most High, magnified and exalted be His glory: "Both Arabic and Persian are laudable. That which is desired of a language is that it convey the intent of the speaker, and either language can serve this purpose. And since in this day the Orb of knowledge hath risen in the firmament of Persia, this tongue deserveth every praise."

The light of truth is indeed shining resplen- 2.58
dent above the horizon of divine utterance, and hence no further elaboration is required from this evanescent soul or from others like unto him. Although there can be no question or doubt as to the sweetness of the Persian tongue, yet it hath not the scope of the Arabic. There are many things which have not been expressed in Persian, that is to say, words referring to such things have not been devised, whilst in Arabic there are several words describing the same thing. Indeed there existeth no language in the world as vast and comprehensive as Arabic. This statement is prompted by truth and fairness; otherwise it is clear that in this day the world is being illumined by the splendours of that Sun which hath dawned above the

horizon of Persia, and that the merits of this sweet language can scarcely be overestimated.

2.59 All the questions of his honour the Ṣáḥib have herewith been mentioned and duly answered. If it be deemed appropriate and advisable, there would be no harm in his perusing these answers himself, and likewise they may be read by the beloved friends in that land, such as Jináb-i-'Alí-Akbar, upon him be the glory of God, the Supreme Ordainer, and Jináb-i-Áqá Mírzá Asadu'lláh, upon him be the Glory of Glories.

2.60 This servant beseecheth the one True God—exalted be His glory—to graciously adorn the world of humanity with justice and fair-mindedness, although in truth the latter is but one of the expressions of the former. Verily, justice is a lamp that guideth man aright amidst the darkness of the world and shieldeth him from every danger. It is indeed a shining lamp. God grant that the rulers of the earth may be illumined by its light. This servant further imploreth God to graciously aid all men to do His will and pleasure. He, in truth, is the Lord of this world and of the world to come. No God is there but Him, the Almighty, the Most-Powerful.

3

Tablet of the Seven Questions

(Lawḥ-i-Haft Pursish)

IN THE NAME OF THE LORD OF UTTERANCE, THE ALL-WISE

ALL PRAISE BE to the sanctified Lord Who 3.1
hath illumined the world through the
splendours of the Daystar of His grace. From the letter "B" He hath made the Most Great Ocean to appear, and from the letter "H" He hath caused His inmost Essence to be made manifest. He is that Almighty One Whose purpose the might of men can never hope to frustrate and the flow of Whose utterance the hosts of kings are powerless to halt.

Thy letter was received, and We perused it 3.2
and heard thy call. Within it were enshrined the precious pearls of love and the hidden mysteries of affection. We beseech the peerless Lord to enable thee to assist His Cause and to lead those who are sore athirst in the wilderness of ignorance to the water of life. His might, in truth,

is equal to all things. That which thou didst ask of the Ocean of Knowledge and the Orb of Insight hath met with His acceptance.

3.3 The first question: "In what tongue and towards what direction doth it behove us to worship the one true God?"

3.4 The beginning of all utterance is the worship of God, and this followeth upon His recognition. Sanctified must be the eye if it is to truly recognize Him, and sanctified must be the tongue if it is to befittingly utter His praise. In this day the faces of the people of insight and understanding are turned in His direction; nay every direction inclineth itself towards Him. O lion-hearted one! We beseech God that thou mayest become a champion in this arena, arise with heavenly power and say: "O high priests! Ears have been given you that they may hearken unto the mystery of Him Who is the Self-Dependent, and eyes that they may behold Him. Wherefore flee ye? The Incomparable Friend is manifest. He speaketh that wherein lieth salvation. Were ye, O high priests, to discover the perfume of the rose garden of understanding, ye would seek none other but Him, and would recognize, in His new vesture, the All-Wise and Peerless One, and would turn your eyes from the world and all who seek it, and would arise to help Him."

The second question concerneth faith and religion. The Faith of God hath in this day been made manifest. He Who is the Lord of the world is come and hath shown the way. His faith is the faith of benevolence and His religion is the religion of forbearance. This faith bestoweth eternal life and this religion enableth mankind to dispense with all else. It verily embraceth all faiths and all religions. Take hold thereof and guard it well. 3.5

The third question: "In what manner shall we deal with the people of this age, who have each chosen to follow a different religion and who each regard their own faith and religion as excelling and surpassing all the others, that we may be shielded from the onslaught of their words and deeds?" 3.6

O lion-hearted one amongst men! Regard the afflictions endured in the path of God as comfort itself. Every affliction suffered for His sake is a potent remedy, every bitterness is naught but sweetness and every abasement an exaltation. Were men to apprehend and acknowledge this truth, they would readily lay 3.7

down their lives for such affliction. For it is the key to inestimable treasures, and no matter how outwardly abhorrent, it hath ever been and will continue to be inwardly prized. We accept and affirm what thou hast said, for the people of the world are indeed bereft of the light of the Orb of justice and regard it as their enemy.

3.8 If thou desirest to be freed from affliction, recite thou this prayer which hath been revealed by the Pen of the All-Merciful: "O God, my God! I testify to Thy unity and to Thy oneness. I beseech Thee, O Thou Possessor of names and Fashioner of the heavens, by the pervasive influence of Thine exalted Word and the potency of Thy supreme Pen, to aid me with the ensigns of Thy power and might, and to protect me from the mischief of Thine enemies who have violated Thy Covenant and Thy Testament. Thou art, verily, the Almighty, the Most Powerful." This invocation is an impregnable stronghold and an indomitable army. It conferreth protection and ensureth deliverance.

3.9 The fourth question: "Our Books have announced that Sháh Bahrám will come, invested with manifold signs, to guide the people aright...."

O friend! Whatsoever hath been announced 3.10
in the Books hath been revealed and made clear. From every direction the signs have been manifested. The Omnipotent One is calling, in this day, and announcing the appearance of the Supreme Heaven. The world hath been illumined with the splendours of His Revelation, yet how few are the eyes that can behold it! Beseech the peerless and incomparable Lord to bestow a penetrating insight upon His servants, for insight leadeth to true knowledge and is conducive to salvation. Indeed, the attainments of man's understanding are dependent upon his keenness of sight. Were the children of men to gaze with the eye of understanding, they would see the world illumined with a new light in this day. Say: The Daystar of knowledge is manifest and the Luminary of insight hath appeared. Fortunate indeed is the one who hath attained, who hath witnessed, and who hath recognized.

The fifth question concerneth the Bridge 3.11
of Ṣirát, Paradise, and Hell. The Prophets of God have come in truth and have spoken the truth. Whatsoever the Messenger of God hath announced hath been and will be made manifest. The world is established upon the foundations

of reward and punishment. Knowledge and understanding have ever affirmed and will continue to affirm the reality of Paradise and Hell, for reward and punishment require their existence. Paradise signifieth first and foremost the good-pleasure of God. Whosoever attaineth His good-pleasure is reckoned and recorded among the inhabitants of the most exalted paradise and will attain, after the ascension of his soul, that which pen and ink are powerless to describe. For them that are endued with insight and have fixed their gaze upon the Most Sublime Vision, the Bridge, the Balance, Paradise, Hellfire, and all that hath been mentioned and recorded in the Sacred Scriptures are clear and manifest. At the time of the appearance and manifestation of the rays of the Daystar of Truth, all occupy the same station. God then proclaimeth that which He willeth, and whoso heareth His call and acknowledgeth His truth is accounted among the inhabitants of Paradise. Such a soul hath traversed the Bridge, the Balance, and all that hath been recorded regarding the Day of Resurrection, and hath reached his destination. The Day of God's Revelation is the Day of the most great Resurrection. We cherish the hope that, quaffing from the choice wine of divine inspiration and the pure waters of heavenly grace, thou mayest attain the station of discovery and witnessing, and behold, both outwardly and inwardly, all that which thou hast mentioned.

The sixth question: "After relinquishing the 3.12
body, that is to say, after the soul hath been separated from the body, it hasteneth to the abode hereafter...."

In reference to this theme there appeared 3.13
some time past from the Pen of divine knowledge that which sufficeth the men of insight and imparteth the greatest joy to the people of understanding. Verily, We say: The soul is gladdened by goodly deeds and profiteth from the contributions made in the path of God.

The seventh question regardeth the name, 3.14
lineage, and ancestry of the Holy One. Abu'l-Faḍl-i-Gulpáygání, upon him be My glory, hath written in this regard, based on the Sacred Scriptures, that which bestoweth knowledge and increaseth understanding.

The Faith of God is endowed with pene- 3.15
trating might and power. Erelong that which hath flowed from Our tongue will outwardly come to pass. We beseech God to bestow upon

thee the strength to assist Him. He, verily, is the All-Knowing, the All-Powerful. Wert thou to obtain and peruse the Súriy-i-Ra'ís and the Súriy-i-Mulúk, thou wouldst find thyself able to dispense with thy questions and wouldst arise to serve the Cause of God in such wise that the oppression of the world and the onslaught of its peoples would fail to deter thee from aiding Him Who is the ancient and sovereign Lord of all.

3.16 We implore God to confirm thee in that which will exalt and immortalize thy name. Make thou an effort, that haply thou mayest obtain the aforementioned Tablets and acquire therefrom a share of the pearls of wisdom and utterance that have issued from the treasury of the Pen of the All-Merciful. The glory of God rest upon thee, upon every steadfast and unwavering heart and upon every constant and faithful soul.

Two Other Tablets

4

THE BEGINNING OF ALL UTTERANCE IS THE PRAISE OF GOD

O SERVANTS! The springs of divine bestowal 4.1
are streaming forth. Quaff ye therefrom, that by the aid of the incomparable Friend ye may be sanctified from this darksome world of dust and enter His abode. Renounce the world and direct your steps toward the city of the Beloved.

O servants! The fire that consumeth all veils 4.2
hath been kindled by My hand; quench it not with the waters of ignorance. The heavens are the token of My greatness; look upon them with a pure eye. The stars bear witness to My truth; bear ye likewise witness thereto.

O servants! Eyes are needed if one is to see, 4.3
and ears, if one is to hear. Whoso in this blessed Day hath not heard the divine call hath indeed no ear. By this is not meant that bodily ear that

is perceived by the eye. Open your inner eye, that ye may behold the celestial Fire, and listen with the ear of inner understanding, that ye may hear the delightsome words of the Beloved.

4.4 O servants! If your heart acheth for the Beloved, lo, the remedy is come! If ye have eyes to see, behold, the shining countenance of the Friend hath appeared! Kindle ye the fire of knowledge and flee from the ignorant. Such are the words of the Lord of the world.

4.5 O servants! Lifeless is the body that is bereft of a soul, and withered the heart that is devoid of the remembrance of its Lord. Commune with the remembrance of the Friend and shun the enemy. Your enemy is such things as ye have acquired of your own inclination, to which ye have firmly clung, and whereby ye have sullied your souls. The soul hath been created for the remembrance of the Friend; safeguard its purity. The tongue hath been created to bear witness to God; pollute it not with the mention of the wayward.

4.6 O servants! Verily I say, he is to be accounted as truthful who hath beheld the straight Path. That Path is one, and God hath chosen and prepared it. It shineth resplendent amongst all paths as the sun amongst the stars. Whosoever hath not attained it hath failed to apprehend the truth and hath gone astray. Such are the counsels of the incomparable, the peerless Lord.

O servants! This nether world is the abode 4.7
of demons: Guard yourselves from approaching them. By demons is meant those wayward souls who, with the burden of their evil deeds, slumber in the chambers of oblivion. Their sleep is preferable to their wakefulness, and their death is better than their life.

O servants! Not every mortal frame hath 4.8
a spirit or is imbued with life. In this day he is endowed with spirit who with all his heart seeketh the abode of the Beloved. The end of all beginnings is to be found in this Day: Turn ye not a blind eye unto it. The matchless Friend is nigh: Stray not far from Him.

O servants! Ye are even as saplings in a garden, 4.9
which are near to perishing for want of water. Wherefore, revive your souls with the heavenly water that is raining down from the clouds of divine bounty. Words must be followed by deeds. Whoso accepteth the words of the Friend is in truth a man of deeds; otherwise a dead carcass is verily of greater worth.

4.10 O servants! Pleasant is the utterance of the Friend: Where is the soul who will taste its sweetness, and where is the ear that will hearken unto it? Well is it with him who, in this day, communeth with the Friend and in His path renounceth and forsaketh all save Him, that he may behold a new world and gain admittance to the everlasting paradise.

4.11 The Lord of the world saith: O servants! Forsake your own desires and seek that which I have desired for you. Walk ye not without one to guide you on the way, and accept ye not the words of every guide. How numerous the guides who have gone astray and failed to discover the straight Path! He alone is a guide who is free from the bondage of this world and whom nothing whatsoever can deter from speaking the truth.

4.12 O servants! Follow the path of truthfulness and turn not away from the needy. Make mention of Me before the great ones of the earth and fear not.

4.13 O servants! Be pure in your deeds, and conduct yourselves in accordance with the words of God. Such are the counsels of the incomparable Lord.

5

THE BEGINNING OF EVERY ACCOUNT IS THE NAME OF GOD

O FRIENDS OF GOD! Incline your inner ears to the voice of the peerless and self-subsisting Lord, that He may deliver you from the bonds of entanglement and the depths of darkness and enable you to attain the eternal light. Ascent and descent, stillness and motion, have come into being through the will of the Lord of all that hath been and shall be. The cause of ascent is lightness, and the cause of lightness is heat. Thus hath it been decreed by God. The cause of stillness is weight and density, which in turn are caused by coldness. Thus hath it been decreed by God. 5.1

And since He hath ordained heat to be the source of motion and ascent and the cause of attainment to the desired goal, He hath therefore kindled with the mystic hand that Fire that 5.2

dieth not and sent it forth into the world, that this divine Fire might, by the heat of the love of God, guide and attract all mankind to the abode of the incomparable Friend. This is the mystery enshrined in your Book that was sent down aforetime, a mystery which hath until now remained concealed from the eyes and hearts of men. That primal Fire hath in this Day appeared with a new radiance and with immeasurable heat. This divine Fire burneth of itself, with neither fuel nor fume, that it might draw away such excess moisture and cold as are the cause of torpor and weariness, of lethargy and despondency, and lead the entire creation to the court of the presence of the All-Merciful. Whoso hath approached this Fire hath been set aflame and attained the desired goal, and whoso hath removed himself therefrom hath remained deprived.

5.3 O servant of God! Turn thou away from the stranger, that thou mayest recognize the Friend. He indeed is a stranger who leadeth you away from the Friend. This is not the day whereon the high priests can command and exercise their authority. In your Book it is stated that the high priests will, on that day, lead men far astray, and will prevent them from drawing nigh unto Him.

He indeed is a high priest who hath seen the light and hastened unto the way leading to the Beloved. Such a man is a benevolent priest and a source of illumination to the whole world.

O servant of God! Any priest who leadeth thee away from this Fire, which is the reality of the Light and the mystery of divine Revelation, is indeed thine enemy. Suffer not the words of the foe to hold thee back from the Friend or the insinuations of the enemy to cause thee to forsake the Beloved. 5.4

O servant of God! The day of deeds hath come: Now is not the time for words. The Messenger of God hath appeared: Now is not the hour for hesitation. Open thou thine inner eye that thou mayest behold the face of the Beloved, and hearken thou with thine inner ear that thou mayest hear the sweet murmur of His celestial voice. 5.5

O servant of God! The robe of divine bestowal hath been sewn and readied. Take hold of it and attire thyself therewith. Renounce and forsake the people of the world. O wise one! Shouldst thou heed the counsel of thy Lord, thou wouldst be released from the bondage of His servants and behold thyself exalted above all men. 5.6

5.7 O servant of God! We have bestowed a dewdrop from the ocean of divine grace; would that men might drink therefrom! We have brought a trace of the sweet melodies of the Beloved; would that men might hearken with their inner ear! Soar upon the wings of joy in the atmosphere of the love of God. Regard the people of the world as dead and seek the fellowship of the living. Whoso hath not breathed the sweet fragrance of the Beloved at this dawntide is indeed accounted among the dead. He Who is the All-Sufficing proclaimeth aloud: "The realm of joy hath been ushered in; be not sorrowful! The hidden mystery hath been made manifest; be not disheartened!" Wert thou to apprehend the surpassing greatness of this Day, thou wouldst renounce the world and all that dwell therein and hasten unto the way that leadeth to the Lord.

5.8 O servants of God! Deprived souls are heedless of this triumphant Day, and chilled hearts have no share of the heat of this blazing Fire.

5.9 O servant of God! The Tree which We had planted with the Hand of Providence hath borne its destined fruit, and the glad-tidings We had imparted in the Book have appeared in full effect.

O servant of God! We revealed Ourself to thee once in thy sleep, but thou didst remain unaware. Remember now, that thou mayest perceive and hasten with heart and soul to the placeless Friend. 5.10

O servant of God! Say: O high priests! The Hand of Omnipotence is stretched forth from behind the clouds; behold ye it with new eyes. The tokens of His majesty and greatness are unveiled; gaze ye on them with pure eyes. 5.11

O servant of God! The Daystar of the everlasting realm is shining resplendent above the horizon of His will and the Oceans of divine bounty are surging. Bereft indeed is the one who hath failed to behold them, and lifeless the one who hath not attained thereunto. Close thine eyes to this nether world, open them to the countenance of the incomparable Friend, and commune intimately with His Spirit. 5.12

O servant of God! With a pure heart unloose thy tongue in the praise of thy Lord for having made mention of thee through His gem-scattering pen. Couldst thou but realize the greatness of this bestowal, thou wouldst find thyself invested with everlasting life. 5.13

NOTES

[1] Iraq.

[2] From the Lawḥ-i-Maqṣúd; cf. *Tablets of Bahá'u'lláh revealed after the Kitáb-i-Aqdas* (Haifa: Bahá'í World Centre, 1988), p. 171.

[3] Qur'án 3:1.

[4] Qur'án 2:285.

[5] Qur'án 2:253.

[6] See 1.4.

[7] The "Necessary Being" (*vájibu'l-vujúd*) refers to God; this term was used by Muslim philosophers such as al-Farabi and can be traced to Aristotle.

[8] *Taqvá*, translated here as "righteousness", has further connotations of piety, fear of God, and right conduct that cannot all be conveyed with a single word in English.

[9] In Islamic law, religious principles (*uṣúl;* lit. "roots") concern the sources of the law that can be explicitly derived from the Qur'án and the Ḥadíth, whereas secondary laws and ordinances (*furú'*; lit. "branches") are deduced from the former through the discipline of jurisprudence (*fiqh*).

[10] Possible reference to Qur'án 2:187, which contains instructions regarding the Fast: "Eat and drink until ye can discern a white thread from a black thread by the daybreak." (Rodwell trans.)

[11] Qur'án 6:91.

[12] Among the rites performed by Muslim pilgrims during the Hajj.

[13] See 1.14.

[14] Muḥammad.

[15] Qur'án 2:143.

[16] See 1.18.

[17] See 1.15.

[18] The "realm of subtle entities" (*'álam-i-dharr*) is an allusion to the Covenant between God and Adam mentioned in Qur'án 7:172. In a Tablet 'Abdu'l-Bahá has written: "The realm of subtle entities that is alluded to referreth to the realities, specifications, individuations, capacities and potentialities of man in the mirror of the divine knowledge. As these potentialities and capacities differ, they each have their own particular exigency. That exigency consisteth in acquiescence and supplication." (*Má'idiy-i-Ásmání*, vol. 2 (New Delhi: Bahá'í Publishing Trust, 1984), p. 30)

[19] Qur'án 2:156.

[20] Qur'án 6:91.

KEY TO PASSAGES TRANSLATED BY SHOGHI EFFENDI

Abbreviation of Sources

GWB Bahá'u'lláh. *Gleanings from the Writings of Bahá'u'lláh.* Wilmette: Bahá'í Publishing Trust, 1994.

KI Bahá'u'lláh. *The Kitáb-i-Íqán.* Wilmette: Bahá'í Publishing Trust, 2003.

PDC Shoghi Effendi. *The Promised Day Is Come.* Wilmette: Bahá'í Publishing Trust, rev. ed., 1996.

Paragraph	*Passage*	*Source*
1.4–1.6	"The All-Knowing Physician… whoso remaineth dead, shall never live."	GWB CVI
1.15	"O well-beloved ones!… and the leaves of one branch."	GWB CXII
2.5	"No distinction do We make between any of His Messengers."	KI ¶161
2.5	"Some of the Apostles We have caused to excel the others."	KI ¶110
2.5	"The All-Knowing Physician… on its exigencies and requirements."	GWB CVI
2.24	"We did not appoint … from him who turneth on his heels."	KI ¶55

2.34	"O ye children of men!... and discord, of hate and enmity."	GWB CX
2.35	"Blessed and happy ... peoples and kindreds of the earth."	GWB CXVII
2.36	"O well-beloved ones!... and the leaves of one branch."	GWB CXII
2.37	"The structure of world stability ... reward and punishment."	GWB CXII
2.51	"Verily, we are God's, and to Him shall we return."	GWB CLXV
2.53	"Say: It is God ... with their cavilings."	KI ¶43
3.4	"O high priests!... and would arise to help Him."	PDC ¶193
3.10	"Whatsoever hath been announced... the Supreme Heaven."	PDC ¶193
5.3	"This is not the day... the way leading to the Beloved."	PDC ¶193
5.11	"O high priests!... gaze ye on them with pure eyes."	PDC ¶193